SLINGSHOTS & KEY HOOKS

SLINGSHOTS & KEY HOOKS

15 everyday objects made from foraged and gathered wood

GEOFFREY FISHER

Photography by

Jake Curtis & Sarah Weal

Fox Chapel Publishing

INTRODUCTION

As far back as I can remember, I've been designing and making things. Whether this impulse took the form of a piece of furniture or an abstract construction, I was always driven by a desire to express myself visually. It was a talent I discovered at an early age, and one I was encouraged to develop both at home and at school, as it was a time when practical subjects were taught as separate lessons and more emphasis was placed on learning a specific skill than there is today. This positive beginning led me to art school, where I learned to work with a wider range of materials and techniques, although wood was what I turned to most often because it had a versatility that few other materials could match.

In the years that followed I never stopped learning about the qualities of wood. By its nature, each piece is unique and therefore uniquely challenging. Technological developments by manufacturers pushed its limits even further, and improvements and innovations in tools meant I could do things with it that I could never do previously. You are joining me at a new stage in this journey, because until recently I mostly worked with prepared timber. A few years ago, however, I discovered the joy of working with wood straight from the tree. My purpose in writing this book is to share this experience with others who are keen to do something creative using natural materials they can source themselves. It seems particularly relevant now, as there is a growing interest from a generation who missed out on the opportunities I was given.

For many reading this book, making a living as a designer-maker, as I have done, is not something they would readily consider, but for the few who might, I'd like to briefly describe my own experience, which has been less than straightforward but certainly not unique. It's well known that to be a commercially successful designer not only requires a level of skill that might take years to achieve, but also a head for business. Most of us possess one but rarely both of these, so sooner or later one of the two has to be learned. With me, the latter was a skill that took some time acquiring, so I had to support my family through teaching and commissions.

Eventually, having a regular income became less of a concern, because I got to a point where the need to do what I loved doing full-time was compelling. Before I took on the responsibilities of a family, I had spent a number of years abroad doing just that, but it was always a struggle, and I didn't want to return to a hand-to-mouth existence.

A compromise had to be made, and that meant I had to design and make things that people actually wanted, not what I thought they wanted. I began by making things for the garden and found there was a positive response. Commissions from garden designers soon followed, which provided a regular income in exchange for producing more conservative designs than perhaps I would have liked. The one thing I was unwilling to compromise on, however, was the quality of work and materials. I felt the rest could follow later, which it did.

Starting off in the years following the financial crisis was a further challenge. A friend with experience in retail suggested that instead of making one-off commissions, I'd be better served making small production runs of handmade products and wholesaling them to shops. I'd had some experience of this before, and knew the percentage mark-up for shops was necessarily high, so it came down to careful costing of materials and efficient production. This was, and still is, a hugely competitive market, so I needed to identify a significant difference between my work and manufactured brands. What I realized I could offer in addition to the quality of the product and its wholesale price was an original design, and this became the focus of the business.

Like so many things that happen to us in life, a chance decision took my relationship with wood in a different direction when a tree in my garden came to the end of its natural life. It was a decision taken for no other reason than I wanted to preserve some small part of it and because one or two branches suggested the shape of hooks. In order to turn these into functional products, the natural shape had to conform to having a straight section with another at an angle suitable for hanging a coat. Although I was unaware of it at the time, the decision to use the shape of the branch to suggest a product was an important change in my design process, one that reversed everything I had done before. Until then, I had started the process of shaping the material with a preconceived design, but now the material determined the design. This discovery provided me with a new and exciting departure from the discipline of my more structured work, a collaborative way of working with nature rather than imposing a design upon it, much as the older generation of woodworkers did when constructing buildings or means of transport. This break from my past meant keeping intervention with the material to a minimum, with the result that selecting a suitable shape became the most important part of the process.

Shortly after this discovery, I was visiting my old neighborhood near Brick Lane in the East End of London and came across a small shop in Cheshire Street called Mar Mar Co. In conversation with the owners, Marianne Lumholdt and Mark Bedford, I mentioned the hooks I had made, which seemed to capture their interest, and so began a long-standing relationship that has lasted up to the present. Marianne and Mark not only shared with me their years of experience in retail, but also worked with me in their capacity as graphic designers to develop a brand that represented what we were all attempting to achieve. Our first thought was to come up with a recognizable name for this product, and eventually we decided on "Trook," a contraction of "Tree" and "Hook," which fits perfectly with the nature of the product and describes exactly what it does. Part of its attraction is its individual character, but the label that accompanies each one also informs the customer exactly where it comes from, the type of tree, and who made it. I guess it is not the most original product I have made, as I now know of a number of other people who make them, but I know of no other product that brings the customer so close to the source of the material and how it was made.

The commercial success of the Trook inevitably meant I needed to look for a regular supply of wood. Foraging in the woodland near where I live takes me out of the studio most weeks. Nothing I collect is deliberately cut down; it is come upon as a consequence of sustainable coppicing or as a result of a tree coming down in a storm. On occasion, searching for wood takes me to places far away from my studio, and last year I returned to a small island near where I used to live and collected olive wood from trees planted by the Venetians hundreds of years ago, so adding another layer to the story of the Trook.

Soon after the success of the Trook, it became clear that other sections of wood could be developed into products, and so there followed numerous others, some of which are in this book. Many are sold to retail stores in the US, the UK, and other countries. One of the most interesting is the range of brushes that I've developed with the help of the last remaining local brush manufacturer in my area. High Wycombe, in Buckinghamshire, where I live, has a long tradition of furniture making, and this is the reason why most of the woodland in the area is planted with beech trees. With the exception of one or two brands, such as Ercol, the furniture industry has largely disappeared, but for a time it supported a local brush-making industry by supplying them with the material for their handles. The last surviving brush manufacturer now sources its handles from abroad, so my use of locally sourced material has been an unintentional but welcome outcome for our product.

Even after so many years of working with it, wood is still my main source of inspiration and continues to hold a deep satisfaction for me on many levels. It stimulates nearly all of the senses—sight, hearing, touch, and smell—and its versatility is inexhaustible, constrained only by the limits of my own imagination. This intimate knowledge is difficult to describe in words but easier to understand once you have begun to make some of the projects described in this book, which are designed with the beginner in mind.

As a designer and maker of products, I can't help but ask whether we need any more things in our lives and whether the acquisition of more things makes our lives any better. The answer to these questions depends on so much, but there is no doubt in my mind that my customers appreciate the products I make, that they become a useful part of their everyday lives and are commented upon by others, and that the story behind them is retold time and time again. This is an important part of the process for me—a process that starts with a fallen tree that would otherwise be left on the ground and ends as a valued possession in the hands of another. It has never been my intention to simply reproduce a product from the past using traditional materials and traditional methods, but rather to make something that reflects the present. This is the reason for this book, which itself is a reflection of the growing interest in reconnecting with the process of making. My hope is that it will introduce readers to the pleasure of sourcing their own wood and learning how to turn this natural material into a useful, and loved, product.

Much of the enjoyment I get from my work since I discovered the pleasure of working with unseasoned wood is having the opportunity to gather my raw material from some of the most beautiful areas of the countryside, both locally and further away from home. Up until then, the sort of work I produced as a studio-based artist gave me no reason to venture beyond my local timber supplier.

Now that I have been working like this for a number of years, I've found it achieves so much more in so many ways. I find that it connects me directly with the material in its natural state and helps me to learn about the unique qualities of each individual tree. I've even learned that these can be significantly different within the same species, according to the soil conditions and exposure to wind and sunlight. In addition to this, it's always in the back of my mind that I'm making use of something that could end up in the hands of another person on the other side of the world, which will connect them with the maker and place.

Personally, I can't think of a better way of making a living, but before we begin to look at what is needed to make the individual projects, it's worth considering the reasons why so many of us have become interested in the process of making. This interest is entirely understandable when more and more of us are now working at desks doing jobs that might be fulfilling in some ways but in other ways less so. Many of us work in large organizations and see few tangible results for our labors, which can be demoralizing. Others went through the modern educational system and feel they missed out on the sort of practical activities that were taught in schools in the past. As consumers we have become increasingly concerned about what we buy and therefore interested in how it was made. We have always demanded value for money and good quality, but now this isn't enough—now we want to know how something was made, what it was made from, and where it came from. Quite often we are prepared to pay a bit more for products that have been sustainably sourced and ethically produced.

The process of making can stimulate us on many levels, including the sensory, intellectual, and physical, as hopefully you will discover through these projects, beginning with the sourcing of the main material.

GETTING STARTED

All the projects in this book use unseasoned wood, which means it is used in its original state from when the tree was felled. This type of wood is known as greenwood because it still contains a lot of moisture, which would otherwise dry out over time or be forced out in a kiln. It is also much softer than seasoned wood, which means it is much easier to work but is less stable, so it can crack and warp. For these small-scale projects, though, this isn't a problem, and can even add to its appearance.

The second important distinction to make is between varieties of deciduous trees, which are generally varieties of hardwoods, and conifers, which are generally varieties of softwoods. Almost all hardwood can be used because hardwoods are slower growing and produce a denser-grained wood that can be more accurately worked and more finely finished. The exception to this is the yew, which is one of only three native coniferous trees in the UK and whose unique qualities produced the longbow.

The sort of hardwoods needed for these projects are easily available wherever you live; my first attempt to make something was from part of a lilac tree that came down in my garden. A neighbor who saw what I was making then offered me some applewood, and as my interest grew, so did my sources of suitable material. Common varieties of hardwoods like ash, beech, hazel, oak, cherry, birch, walnut, elm, hawthorn, and sycamore are all suitable, but the best way to tell is by testing them out and seeing for yourself.

If your local neighborhood doesn't provide you with the wood you need, then you can begin to look further afield, but there are a number of important issues that should be considered before you begin. The main thing to bear in mind is getting permission to collect from whoever owns the wood; otherwise this can lead to problems.

Your first thought might be to visit a local park or public wood after a storm to collect branches from a fallen tree, but this can lead to you being accused of theft if you haven't spoken to the person responsible for maintaining the area. The ecology of such areas is very carefully monitored, so unless you are aware of what goes on, you could be unintentionally responsible for causing damage or spreading disease.

Provided you contact the person responsible for the land, they will seldom refuse permission if you explain exactly what you are doing. You need to give them the reassurance that you are only interested in collecting small quantities of wood already on the ground that have no commercial value and emphasize that you have no intention of damaging a living tree. I only collect what I can carry out on foot

in a bag and only use hand saws so as to have the minimum negative impact on the environment. If you also explain what you are intending to use the wood for, they are usually very pleased to see what might be a waste material being put to good use.

It goes without saying that you should conduct yourself responsibly and leave the area as you found it or even better. I frequently pick up other people's litter and dispose of it appropriately. As a precautionary measure, if you are working on your own, always let someone else know where you are and make sure you have a fully charged phone should you need help, as it is easy to have a fall, especially if you are working on uneven ground. After having had a minor accident, I now carry a small first aid kit and, in areas of poor mobile phone reception, a map, as it is surprisingly easy to get disoriented when absorbed in searching for a particular shape or size of a branch. Appropriate outer clothing and, more importantly, appropriate footwear is another consideration, as casual shoes might be all right on well-trodden woodland paths but not when you wander off into the undergrowth.

Privately owned areas of commercial woodland are some of the best-maintained and can be a valuable source of material. Having access to these areas depends upon getting permission from the owner and then building a relationship with them, showing respect for what has been achieved. Maintaining a healthy woodland is expensive and sometimes requires the removal of perfectly healthy trees to allow the remainder to grow. Unseasoned hardwood can also be obtained by contacting local tree surgeons who often work in domestic neighborhoods and may be able to provide you with varieties that are more unusual than those found in public or private woodland.

You should also be aware that rules about felling trees vary widely depending on country, state, city, season, and type of tree. Make sure that you have done your research and have any necessary permits before cutting back or felling any trees..

Once you have found a reliable source of wood and gained permission to collect it, you might find that on closer examination not everything can be used. This is something that is learned through experience, but it is also, to some extent, a matter of choice. In my case, I only collect wood that has recently fallen, because anything that has been on the ground for more than a few months will have deteriorated. On the other hand, learning the way to identify different varieties of hardwoods isn't a matter of choice but a necessity, and this can come from either a well-illustrated, well-written handbook or some other source such as an online source.

The first thing you will notice when identifying a variety of hardwood is the distinctive appearance of the bark; something like cherry, which has markings going around the branch, is different from oak, which has markings going along the branch. Birch has similar markings to cherry but is different in color. In winter, with the absence of leaves, I still found the difference between ash and sycamore difficult to identify until someone told me that ash has black buds and sycamore has white ones. Of course, leaf shape and color is another reliable way to tell the difference between varieties of hardwoods, and as a matter of interest, the presence of lichens can show areas of clean air, which is good to know.

The size and shape of what you are intending to make will also play a part in what you decide to take away, but sometimes I collect something with no specific purpose in mind, only because it has grown into an interesting shape. This purpose might gently reveal itself later, and this is my preferred way of working, because my aim is to minimize the influence of the human hand and maximize the shape created by nature.

One area of knowledge I developed over the years could not have been taught. I've found that I can tell the condition of a branch by its appearance and weight. If the bark is beginning to fragment and change color, these are signs that rainwater has penetrated and begun to weaken the structure, making it unsuitable for my purposes. If it feels comparatively light, again the chances are it has started to deteriorate and will not respond well when worked. The sound and feeling transmitted by the saw when cutting is another good sign of what to select and what to reject. This initial selection avoids waste.

When working in an area with public access, your activities may draw the attention of other people. Usually they will pass by without comment. Very occasionally I've found myself being questioned and have had to explain what I am doing and that I've been granted permission. Most then move on, but sometimes I'm challenged further. At this point, I find myself explaining that coppicing is a necessary part of maintaining woodland, as it ensures larger trees have more room to develop and also brings a valuable source of sunlight to the woodland floor, which enables wild flowers to grow.

Lastly, be prepared for the unexpected. In my case, "unexpected" mainly means dogs allowed to wander off the path. One dog decided to relieve itself over my woodpile and another to steal a particularly choice piece of wood as soon as it dropped to the floor after being cut!

TOOLS AND EQUIPMENT

A friend's daughter once accused him of having *all the gear but no idea* when he was about to leave the house for his first skiing lesson dressed up in his recent purchases. There is of course something to this remark, as it is very tempting to buy everything you could possibly need when you take up a new interest but before you've developed the necessary skills to carry it through. I guess everyone does this to a lesser or greater extent, but all it gives is a false sense of achievement. Real achievement comes much harder and slower and certainly can't be bought over the internet, so I'd suggest you begin with a few essential purchases, then add to these as and when needed.

With the exception of one or two regrettable purchases, I buy the best-quality tools I can afford, as they will last more than a lifetime and can be passed on. It's also good advice for someone starting out to make sure that the tools you buy are the right ones for the job, as anything else can cause damage to the work or the user. Very early on I was told that a blunt tool is more dangerous than a sharp one, which turns out to be true, as a blunt tool will need more force behind it, which can lead to less control.

TOOLS **1.** Small Round Rasp **2.** Steel Rulers **3.** Pencil **4.** Permanent Marker/Pen **5.** Screwdriver **6.** Japanese Sanding Plate Tool **7.** Sanding Disc **8.** Two-Part Epoxy Glue **9.** Scissors **10.** Plastic-Faced Mallet

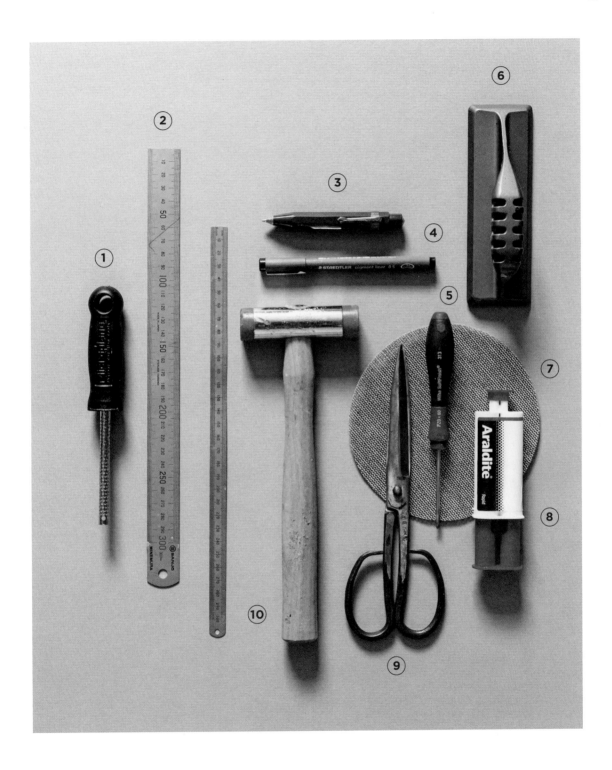

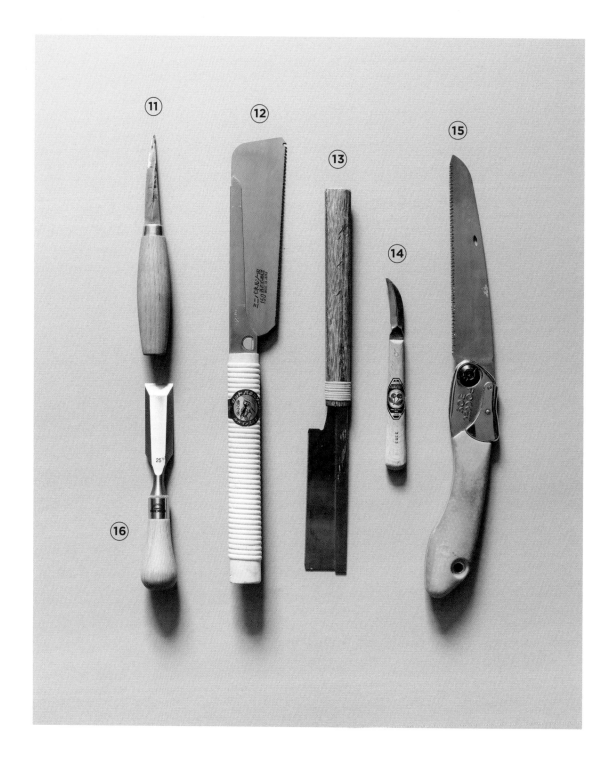

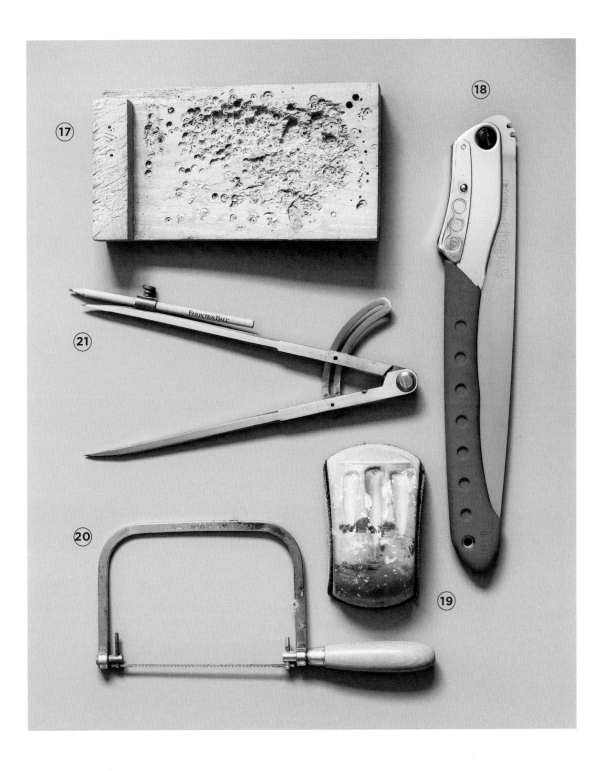

It's not an exaggeration to say that anyone who is serious about the process of making builds a personal relationship with their tools, because they are the means by which you create something that could not be achieved in any other way. This is why choosing the correct tool for the job is so important and the satisfaction that comes from using a tool that perfectly performs a particular task is second to none.

Technological developments over the years have improved the quality and performance of traditional hand tools enormously, although essentially they are doing the same work they always did, but better.

TIP

Do not mix imperial and metric measurements when creating the projects in this book. Not all equivalents are identical, but each projects' measurements are self-consistent within both the imperial and metric measurements given.

TOOLS (PICTURED ON PAGE 28–29) 11. Woodcarving Knife
12. Japanese Pull Saw 13. Japanese Fine-Toothed Pull Saw
14. Chip Carving Knife 15. Japanese Medium-Toothed Pruning Saw
16. Single-Bevel Carpenter's Chisel 17. Bench Hook
18. Japanese Large-Toothed Pruning Saw 19. Sanding Block
20. Coping Saw 21. Compass

22. Portable Bench Vise 23. Brad Point Woodworking Bits 24. Forstner Bit
25. Countersink 26. Tenon Cutter 27. Variable Speed Cordless Drill

31

PLACE CARD HOLDER

Place card holders can be useful for all sorts of occasions—to indicate the seating arrangements at weddings, birthday parties, corporate events, or private dinner parties. The design for this place card holder is slightly different from most others and will readily be commented on by your guests. Alternatively, it can be used to display a cherished family photograph, a recently purchased postcard, or a reminder note on a desk. This project involves a number of skills that may take some practice to get right but are worth the effort in the end, as you will have made something to be proud of and that will be appreciated by others. Any variety of hardwood would be suitable, and the size can be a matter of personal choice, although the diameter of the tenon cutter will have some restrictions on that.

TOOLS
Bench Vise, ¾" (19mm) Tenon Cutter, Cordless Drill, Japanese Fine-Toothed Pull Saw, ¼" (6mm) Brad Point Woodworking Bit, Sanding Block, Bench Hook, Pull Saw, Wide Single-Bevel Carpenter's Chisel

MATERIALS
Ash, Hazel, Beech, Sycamore, Yew, Cherry, Oak, or Birch
Length of ¼" (6mm) diameter Slingshot Elastic Tubing

CUTTING THE TOP

The safest way to make the top is to cut an oversized length of greenwood so it can be firmly held in the vise and then cut it to the finished size at a later stage.

Ensure that the drill holding the tenon cutter is in line with the section of greenwood both from the side and top and that it is held securely in the bench vise. Before you start the cut, the drill should be set to slow. If using a variable-speed drill, start slow and then increase the speed as the cut is made to form the tenon.

As this is such a small item, it's worth taking care to get a smooth cut, as any imperfection will be obvious. If you have any problems in operating the tenon cutter, then refer back to the detailed instructions included with the tool.

VERTICAL CUT

This vertical cut needs precision and can only be achieved by eye as there is no easy way to take a measurement. I've used a Japanese fine-toothed pull saw, which helps make a straight cut and only removes the minimum amount of wood. The cut should be made to the estimated finished height.

DRILLING

In this project I'm using ¼" (6mm) diameter slingshot elastic tubing, so an equivalent diameter drill bit is needed. Using a brad point woodworking drill bit is particularly advisable in this instance because it helps to make an accurate hole with the minimum of splintering when it breaks through on the opposite side. This can be entirely avoided if you drill until you can just see the drill bit point appear, then stop and drill in from the other side to produce a completely clean hole.

ROUNDING THE TOP EDGES

Before you separate the two halves, the top can be rounded over by eye with a sanding block, then you can gently remove the edge to form a neat chamfer.

SEPARATING THE TWO HALVES

It's much easier to remove the work from the vise and use the bench hook to make the cut across the grain to separate the two halves. This cut needs to be made at right angles to the height to form a base that will not fall over when used.

SMOOTHING THE INSIDES

Even a fine saw blade will produce some roughness, so you will need to smooth down the inner surfaces with a sanding block.

CUTTING THE TAPER

If you've not had much practice with working with a chisel, it's worth making sure it is in good condition and held firmly against the bench hook. The chisel I've used is quite wide, which gives a cleaner cut, and the objective is to remove enough material to form a taper from the middle to the base. It will help if you you have in mind the mechanism of a wooden clothes pin.

ATTACHING THE ELASTIC TUBING

The elastic tubing I've used here I bought
online from a supplier of slingshot
components. It comes in different colors and
diameters, but ¼" (6mm) seems to work well
with this size of place card holder. Threading
the tubing through the hole can be slightly
difficult, so it is best to hold it in the vise so
both hands are free. Once you have secured
one end with a simple knot, the tubing needs
to be stretched to the maximum before you
secure the other end with a similar knot. For
this reason, I prefer to have a long length
of tubing to pull through, as you can get a
better grip than when using a shorter length.

TIP

You might find that once you have been
gathering material for a while, each place
card holder could be made from a different
variety of hardwood, which would make
yet another feature to be commented
upon by your guests.

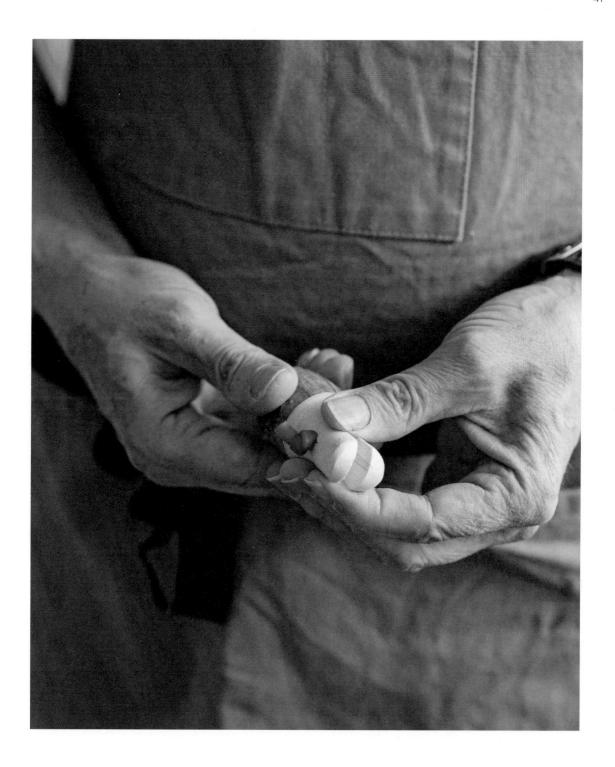

HOOK

This is probably the simplest and yet most useful of all the projects in this book and the one that remains my favorite even now, as it was the first in line of what followed when I began discovering the pleasure of going out into the woods and turning what I gathered into something useful for other people. I sometimes get asked if these hooks, or "Trooks" as they became known, would be strong enough to support a weight. When you think about it, even a small branch of a tree is designed to support any number of leaves, and when it rains or snows it supports even more. To make our hook, we are using the strength of the branch at its strongest point, so it is more than capable of supporting the heaviest of items.

TOOLS
Bench Hook, Pull Saw, Bench Vise, Sanding Block, Cordless Drill, ³⁄₁₆" (5mm) Brad Point Woodworking Bit, Countersink Bit

MATERIALS
Ash, Beech, Sycamore, Yew, Cherry, Oak, or Birch
Two Wood Screws

SELECTING THE WOOD

The only criteria to selecting a suitable shape to make a hook is to identify a straight section of the branch that could form the back so it can be attached flat against a wall. Apart from that, you have the opportunity with this project to use many of the unique shapes and sizes of branches that nature offers you, including some that could make double or triple hooks.

CUTTING TO SIZE

Depending on what branches you have selected as possible hooks, you can now begin to cut them to size according to their height and distance from the wall or door. You might have a specific purpose in mind or decide to leave that decision until later, when you see the results.

For most cuts, it is advisable to use the pull saw and bench hook, but for more awkward and often more interesting shapes the bench vise is a safer option, to avoid any accidents.

FORMING THE BACK

Much of the appeal of these hooks is their shape, which means that they don't conform to normal methods of measuring and marking out, so this has to be achieved by eye. To form the back of the hook you will need to decide where it is possible to make a straight saw cut and then secure the work in the bench vise. Because you will be cutting along the grain as opposed to across it, there is a tendency for the saw to get stuck, which is why I've used a saw with a thicker blade.

FINISHING

The back of your hook is going to be quite rough from the saw cut, so you will need to smooth this out so that later it can be properly secured against the flat surface of a wall or door. Unseasoned hardwood has the tendency to clog the surface of abrasive papers, so a coarser grit might be best used in the initial stage with a finer grit to finish. The ends can then be rounded over and chamfered.

DRILLING THE SCREW HOLE

The size of these holes will depend upon the size of the hook, so all you need to do is take this into consideration. One central hole top and bottom is sufficient, which are then finished with the countersink bit so the screw heads are safely out of the way, below the surface of the branch.

MAGNETIC HOOK

A magnetic hook can be useful to hold a light object on a metal surface, such as an oven mitt on a stainless-steel splashback. Apart from being a practical item, the appearance of these two contrasting materials makes an interesting feature that at first glance takes you by surprise. By following the instructions on pages 42–46 and successfully making a hook but stopping before drilling the screw holes, you are ready to attach two magnets to the back so it can be used against metal surfaces. Magnets come in all sorts of shapes, sizes, and strengths, but using magnets with countersunk holes that take a wood screw is a good way of ensuring they can be secured to the back of the hook.

TOOLS
Bench Vise, Pull Saw, Bench Hook, Sanding Block, Cordless Drill, ⅜" (10mm) Forstner Bit, Awl, Screwdriver

MATERIALS
Ash, Beech, Sycamore, Yew, Cherry, Oak, or Birch
Two Countersunk Magnets, Two Wood Screws

ATTACHING THE MAGNETS

Before making a start with attaching the
magnets to the prepared hook, it is important
to make sure the back of your hook is entirely
flat so the magnets will have good contact
with a metal surface. Once you are satisfied
then you need to mark out the positions
top and bottom for two holes. The magnets
shown here are ⅜" (10mm) in diameter by
1/16" (2mm) thick and they require a clean,
shallow hole; a ⅜" (10mm) diameter forstner
bit is best suited to this purpose. When
drilling the holes the forstner bit needs to be
at right angles to the work, which should be
held securely in the bench vise. Lastly, place
the magnets in the holes and make pilot
holes with an awl to take the screws.

COBWEB BRUSH

For anyone who finds housework a less than enjoyable experience, the ownership of a cobweb brush could be the first step along the road to turning this chore into something more acceptable. In addition to some small sections of greenwood used to make the handle and stock (see page 54), this project involves the use of coconut fiber, which is a natural fiber extracted from the husk of the coconut palm. Coconut fiber has a multitude of uses in addition to brush-making, and is a sustainable alternative to animal or synthetic fiber.

TOOLS
Bench Vise, Cordless Drill, ⅝" (15mm) Fortsner Bit, ⅜" (10mm) Brad Point Woodworking Bit, Pull Saw, Bench Hook, Sanding Block, Scissors

MATERIALS
Ash, Hazel, Beech, Sycamore, Yew, Cherry, Oak, or Birch
Coconut Fiber, ⅜" (10mm) Dowel, Plastic Funnel, Two-Part Epoxy Glue, Rubber Bands, Length of Leather Lace

MAKING THE STOCK

In brush-making, the part of the brush that holds the fibers together is called the stock, and here you'll need a length of greenwood approximately 5" (125mm) long and 1" (25mm) thick for this purpose. This is longer than the finished size, but this length makes it easier to hold the brush during the next step.

Securing the work in the bench vise, and using a ⅝" (15mm) diameter forstner bit, drill the first hole to a depth of ⅝" (15mm). The second and third holes should be drilled to the same depth at either side of the first but at a slight angle to allow the coconut fibers to spread out when glued into place.

A length of dowel is going to be used to join the stock to the handle, so drill a ⅜" (10mm) hole in the reverse side, then cut the stock to length using the pull saw and bench hook.

MAKING THE HANDLE

This can be made from a similar length and thickness of greenwood as the stock. Hold it securely in the bench vise and drill another ⅜" (10mm) hole for the dowel.

FINISHING THE SURFACES AND EDGES

Both the stock and handle need their ends finished with the sanding block to remove any surface marks caused by the saw cuts.

The edges can be treated in a similar way to the ends to avoid splintering.

MAKING THE KNOTS

Coconut fiber comes in pre-prepared lengths called hanks; when it is divided up to make a brush, this is called a knot, which is then glued into the stock.

Making a knot by hand from coconut fiber can be difficult, so one way of making it easier is to cut off part of a plastic funnel so the opening corresponds to the size of the knot. By forcing the coconut fiber through the opening in the funnel and then securing it with rubber bands at both ends, a ⅝" (15mm) knot can be made.

ASSEMBLING THE COMPONENTS

Assembling the finished components can be done in any order, but I've chosen to start by first gluing the dowel into the stock and then the handle. If you want to be able to hang up the cobweb brush, you could add a leather loop by drilling a hole through the handle at the top.

Using the bench vise—so that you can use both hands—glue the coconut fiber knots into the stock with a two-part epoxy glue.

FINISHING TOUCHES

It is best to leave the epoxy glue to fully cure overnight before removing the rubber bands from the coconut fiber knots.

Once the epoxy glue has fully cured, remove any loose coconut fibers and trim the ends with scissors to make a pleasing shape.

TIP

The processes shown in this project can be used to make other types of brushes, so there is an opportunity here to make one for a specific purpose of your own choice.

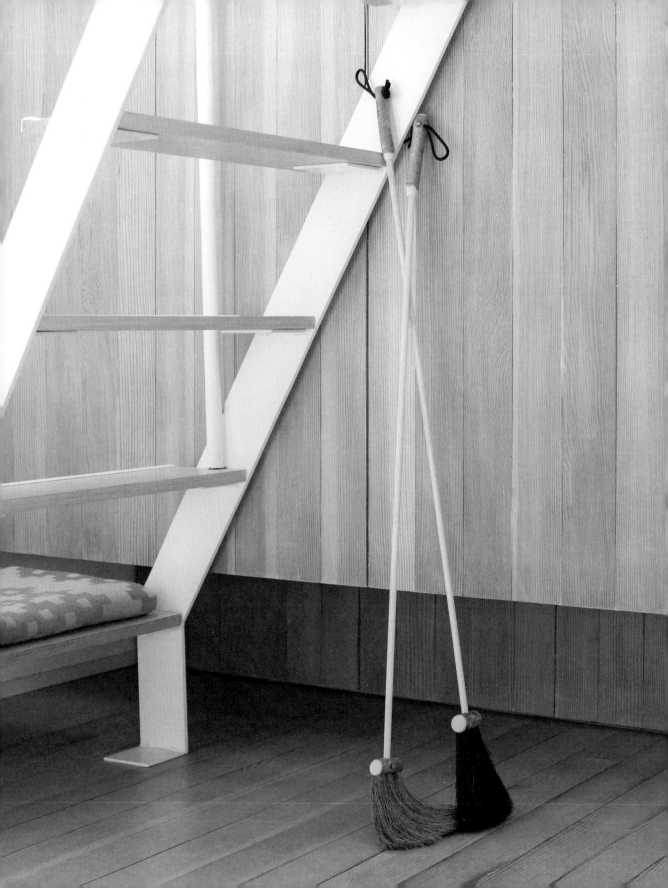

KEY FOB

This project will enable you to make good use of some of the most interesting shapes and sizes of unseasoned hardwood pieces that you might otherwise leave behind when out gathering. It can also give you the chance to use varieties of less-common hardwoods and to learn about their individual characteristics. These unique qualities can be used to identify keys for different purposes or ownership, so there is no longer an excuse for loss or confusion.

TOOLS

Bench Vise, Tenon Cutter, Pull Saw, Cordless Drill, ³⁄₁₆" (5mm) Brad Point Woodworking Bit, Countersink Bit, Sanding Block, Bench Hook

MATERIALS

Ash, Hazel, Beech, Sycamore, Yew, Cherry, Oak, or Birch
Brass Split Ring, Length of Leather Lace

SHAPING THE END

With the work held securely in the bench vise, the end can be neatly made using a tenon cutter (see page 36 for instructions). The tenon cutter exposes the inner grain of the wood, which contrasts well with the texture of the bark, making an interesting feature along with the shape.

In summer, when trees are in leaf and the sap is rising, it is possible to remove all the bark by hand and expose the tactile bone-like quality along the entire length.

ATTACHING THE SPLIT RING

This next stage takes a bit of care because drilling the hole to attach the split ring can cause the end to splinter. This can be avoided if you stop drilling once the point of the brad point bit appears on the opposite side of the work, then turn it over and resume drilling. Attach the split ring. Then drill another hole at the opposite end of the key fob in the same way, countersink the holes, and attach a short length of leather. As both holes are countersunk, the split ring and leather can move smoothly. Using the sanding block, smooth over the edges and finally attach the split ring.

CLOTHES HANGER

A clothes hanger is one of those classic pieces of modern design that is recognizable across the world. Although the basic triangular shape remains the same, there are three types of clothes hangers you could make—the simplest is made from twisted wire, or there are those made from wood and plastic. The clothes hanger in this project might bear some resemblance to the bought ones you have in your closet, but by the very nature of the material you are going to use, the finished work will look like no other. In this example, I decided to use some pieces of sycamore that I collected when the tree was in leaf, when they could be easily stripped of the bark to reveal a bone-like surface that was smooth to the touch and so ideal for hanging clothes on. If you decide to make a hanger with the bark left on, any of the suggested species would be suitable as long as the surface is not too rough for use—otherwise it will damage your clothes.

TOOLS
Bench Vise, Bench Hook, Pull Saw, Pencil, Ruler, Cordless Drill, Tenon Cutter, ⅛" (3mm) and ⅜" (10mm) Brad Point Woodworking Bits, Sanding Block, Countersink Bit, Screwdriver

MATERIALS
Ash, Hazel, Beech, Sycamore, Yew, Cherry, Oak, or Birch
Two-Part Epoxy Glue, Two ⅛" (3mm) Countersunk Wood Screws, Galvanized Screw Hook, Wood Screws

SELECTING THE WOOD

You will need three different thicknesses of greenwood to make this project, the first of which will form the central component. This central component needs to be cut from a piece of greenwood approximately 1¾" (45mm) thick and 1⅛" (30mm) in length. The second thickness you will need forms the arms, and the third the crossbar. Both need to be reasonably straight and should measure approximately ⅝" (15mm) and ⅜" (10mm) respectively in thickness.

MEASURING THE ARMS

Before cutting the tenons, you need to measure the length of the arms by using an existing clothes hanger as a template. You should allow a little extra wood for the arm tenons.

Following the instructions in the place card holder project on page 36, make a tenon at one end of each of the arms.

I used a ⅜" (10mm) tenon cutter to make these joints, so I needed to drill two holes to form the mortices using a ⅜" (10mm) brad point drill bit. These mortices need to be drilled in two separate stages to accurately calculate the angle between the arms.

The first one should be drilled at right angles along one side of the central component to the estimated depth of the tenon.

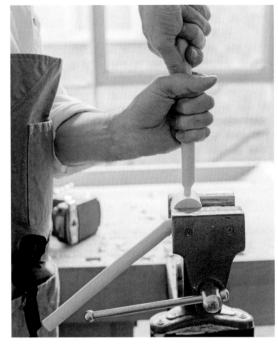

JOINING THE ARMS

Taking one of the tenons, cut it to length so that it is no longer than the depth of the mortise. Once this has been done, it can be glued into place and left to dry. You are now ready to calculate the angle at which you need to drill the second mortise, by securing the work in the bench vise and once again using an existing clothes hanger as a template. Position the work in the bench vise so a second mortise can be drilled from an upright position.

The second tenon can then be cut to length and glued into place.

PREPARING THE CROSSBAR

Mark the cuts needed to fit the crossbar by holding the piece in position and drawing a pencil line at each end.

Using the bench hook and pull saw, cut the crossbar to length, then drill a screw clearance hole in each end with a ⅛" (3mm) brad point bit.

Before permanently fitting the crossbar into position, smooth over all edges with the sanding block.

FITTING THE CROSSBAR

While holding one end of the crossbar into position, permanently secure the other end with a ⅛" (3mm) countersunk wood screw, and then permanently secure the remaining end.

FITTING THE SCREW HOOK

The screw hook needs to be positioned centrally at a right angle into the central component so it balances well when hung up on a rail. To avoid splitting, drill a pilot hole slightly smaller than the diameter of the screw hook, and then carefully screw it in.

TIP

This design could be easily adapted for other purposes, such as displaying kitchen utensils. Alternatively, by scaling it up and adding a second crossbar, it could be used to hold towels.

BEE HOTELS

Most people are familiar with the honey bees and bumble bees that live in colonies, but the majority of the bees that are native to North America (and elsewhere) are known as solitary bees and are amazingly effective pollinators. Solitary bees are highly diverse, and so are their nesting habits. The majority nest in the ground by excavating their own holes where the female then lays her egg. The mason bee is a familiar sight in the US, and this species will quickly set up home in a bee hotel like this one. It is important that once you have made your bee hotel it is positioned in full sun and at least 3' (1m) above the ground with no vegetation obscuring the entrance, otherwise it is unlikely to be used.

TOOLS
Bench Vise, Pull Saw, Cordless Drill, ⅜" (9mm) Brad Point Woodworking Bit, Countersink Bit, Sanding Block, Bench Hook, Plastic-Faced Mallet, Screwdriver

MATERIALS
Ash, Hazel, Beech, Sycamore, Yew, Cherry, Oak, or Birch
Wood Screws, ³⁄₁₆" (4mm) Dowel

SELECTING THE WOOD

Any type of greenwood can be used to make a bee hotel as long as it is reasonably straight. Each piece should be longer than the length of a drill bit and no more than about ¾" (a couple of centimeters) thick. Once you have selected your pieces of wood, make the cut at a slight angle to provide an overhang above the hole you will drill next, to protect the bee from rainfall when the wood is mounted into position.

DRILLING

Some bee hotels fail to attract inhabitants because the holes are too large—a hole of ⅜" (9mm) diameter or less is recommended.

Secure the work in the bench vise and drill a hole down the center as far as the drill bit will allow, then drill a second, smaller hole from the other end for the mounting screw.

COUNTERSINKING

It is important that the entrance is smooth and free of splinters—as well as the entire length of the hole—otherwise the bee will damage its wings. Use the countersink bit around the entrance to the hole, then drill a hole where you want to attach the perch.

FITTING THE PERCH

If you use a piece of dowel the same diameter as the hole, the perch will require no gluing to secure it.

Once the perch is fixed into position, cut it to length and smooth the edges. The bee hotel is now ready to receive guests. Remember to screw it in place in full sun at least 3' (1m) above the ground.

TIP

A perch is not entirely necessary, and as there is no evidence that a perch will attract a prospective inhabitant looking for a desirable place to lay an egg, it can easily be omitted.

PLANT MARKERS

Whether you are starting seeds outdoors or transplanting new seedlings into the garden, it can be easy for gardeners to mix up what went where. Plant markers are a helpful reminder of what you planted and where, and what can be better than making some either for yourself or as a gift. If you decide to make them for your personal use, the diameter and length of the wood you select can be determined by the sort of planting you intend to do; otherwise, just use whatever is available. Any variety of unseasoned hardwood can make a suitable plant marker, but with this project there is an opportunity to use some imagination in terms of shape, as there is no reason why they should be entirely straight. If you are planning to make them as a gift, how about making each one from a different hardwood variety to showcase the local tree population in your area?

TOOLS
Bench Hook, Pull Saw, Bench Vise, Cordless Drill, Tenon Cutter, Small Round Rasp, Wide Single-Bevel Carpenter's Chisel, Sanding Block, Permanent Marker/Pen

MATERIALS
Ash, Hazel, Beech, Sycamore, Yew, Cherry, Oak, or Birch

SELECTING THE WOOD

Choosing pieces of wood that are suitable for making plant markers depends on what is available and what their intended use might be. If you are planning to place them where you have planted a row of beans, the markers will need to be of a longer length than if you are labeling herbs in a window box.

CUTTING TO LENGTH

Using a pull saw, hold the work firmly against the top edge of the bench hook and cut to the appropriate size. If your aim is to make several plant markers of the same length, use one as a template and mark all the others accordingly.

SHAPING THE ENDS

The end of the plant marker that is going into the soil can be neatly made using a tenon cutter provided you follow the detailed instructions included with each tool (see page 36). At the opposite end you will need to remove a section of wood on which you can write the name of the plant. This can be done by cutting a shoulder with a small round rasp to the depth of approximately one-third of the thickness to retain a degree of strength. Using a slicing action with a sharp, wide chisel, remove more wood until the required depth is reached.

FINISHING THE EDGES

To finish off both ends of your plant markers, you can make a chamfer by using a sanding block held at an approximately forty-five-degree angle to the edges. This not only improves the appearance of the marker, but also prevents splintering.

NAMING YOUR PLANTS

Depending on whether or not your plant markers are for personal use or a gift, you may want to handwrite the names using a permanent marker/pen. Once they have served their purpose, at the end of the season they can be resurfaced and reused.

TIP

A simple alternative to using a tenon cutter for shaping the end of the plant marker that goes into the soil is a traditional woodcarving knife, which will always be a useful addition to your tool collection.

DIBBER

For anyone interested in gardening, a dibber is one of those tools that has a number of uses and, in this case, can be easily adapted for a specific person or purpose. For a young person planting a row of seeds in a seed tray, the proportions will be different than those needed by an older person who wants to plant bulbs in a lawn. If you are an enthusiastic gardener or you know somebody who is, you may want to make a range of dibbers for different purposes, or make one in response to a particular need when necessary. An essential component of this project is to teach you how to join two sections of greenwood at right angles to each other. This is a traditional woodworking joint known as a mortise and tenon, which is made up of two components: the mortise hole and the tenon tongue. With some imagination, you could use the same woodworking joint to make other products.

TOOLS

Bench Vise, Tenon Cutter, Cordless Drill, Bench Hook, Pull Saw, Brad Point Woodworking Bit, Sanding Block, Countersink Bit

MATERIALS

Ash, Hazel, Beech, Sycamore, Yew, Cherry, Oak, or Birch
Two-Part Epoxy Glue, Length of Leather Lace

SELECTING THE WOOD

The greenwood you need for this project depends upon the intended purpose and person, but it will need to be relatively straight to make a strong joint.

CUTTING THE JOINT

Joining two sections of greenwood together at right angles is a simple process provided you carefully follow the instructions included with each tool. Make sure the tenon you cut is straight and central; otherwise it will not fit comfortably into the mortise.

Once you have made the tenon, you can separate the handle and drill a hole halfway along with a brad point bit of the same size to make the mortise. This hole should be drilled at right angles to the handle; then, as soon as the point emerges on the opposite side, stop drilling.

ASSEMBLING THE JOINT

Before you finally assemble the joint, the tenon may need to be trimmed to length so it is not longer than the depth of the mortise. Once this has been done, it can be glued into place and left to dry, which should take an hour or two.

FINISHING

You may want to finish the end of your dibber by smoothing off the edges with a sanding block, then doing the same with the ends of the handle. An alternative is to make another cut with the tenon cutter to the depth you want to plant and then sand the end.

If you want to hang up the dibber, drill and countersink a small hole in the handle and thread through a short length of leather lace.

SLINGSHOT

For a certain generation, a slingshot conjures up memories of a time when children made their own and played with them on nearby fields or in woods. In comics of a bygone era, slingshots were invariably seen tucked into the back pocket of a misbehaving boy, and were the cartoonists' shorthand for outdoor fun and adventure. As long as they are used responsibly, they can be a much-loved outdoor essential. In addition to such games as shooting at cans and bottles, a slingshot is a practical way to launch seedballs onto inaccessible rough ground or fishing bait into water. The aim of this project is to make a slingshot that is both fun and safe to use; it should never be used as a weapon or aimed at either people or animals.

TOOLS
Bench Hook, Pull Saw, Bench Vise, Sanding Block, Cordless Drill, ⁵⁄₁₆" (8mm) Brad Point Woodworking Bit, ⁵⁄₁₆" (8mm) Drill Bit, Countersink Bit

MATERIALS
Ash, Beech, Sycamore, Yew, Cherry, Oak, or Birch
Two ¼" x 1⅛" (6mm x 30mm) Pre-Cut Beech Dowels, ⁵⁄₁₆" (8mm) Spare Slingshot Elastic Tubing (this can be obtained from fishing equipment suppliers), Pouch, Leather Lace

SELECTING THE WOOD

The first step is to find a suitably shaped branch that forms a natural division and is also roughly symmetrical. This can be more difficult than it sounds, but it's worth persisting until you find something of the right size and shape, as it needs to fit comfortably in the hand and be strong enough to withstand the pressure of the elastic tubing.

For reasons that will be explained later, each fork needs to measure at least ¾" (20mm) in diameter. Most hardwoods—such as beech, ash, sycamore, and oak—are suitable, but whatever wood is chosen, it is essential that it is put through some initial testing to see if it will withstand the sort of pressure the elastic tubing can apply.

Don't use wood that has been left on the woodland floor for any length of time, as rainwater is likely to have worked its way through to the main core and weakened it.

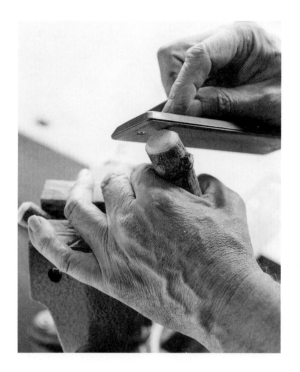

TRIMMING THE WOOD TO SIZE

Once a suitable branch has been chosen, work can begin to fashion a slingshot that fits the size of the intended user's hand. One way of achieving this is to grasp the handle end of the branch and take a measurement of the hand's width, then repeat it along the remaining forks.

SMOOTHING OVER THE ENDS

Even the finest saw will produce a rough finish, so the first step in finishing the slingshot ends is to smooth off each surface with an abrasive tool while the slingshot is held in the vise. This can be further improved by chamfering the edges at an angle, which reduces the chance of splintering where the bark meets the heartwood.

DRILLING HOLES

This is the part of the process that needs the most care and accuracy, as it is important when drilling the holes not to weaken the structure of the forks. The elastic tubing I've chosen is 5⁄16" (8mm) in diameter, so it will need the same-size hole drilled with a brad point type bit so it doesn't drift. The hole centers should be approximately 1" (25mm) apart. Once drilled, test the fork to make certain it will not break under pressure. If it breaks during testing, discard the wood and replace with a larger-diameter fork. The process should be repeated until you are satisfied the fork will withstand the pressure of fully extended elastic tubing. To avoid any possible damage to the tubing on the edges of the hole, they should be countersunk to a depth of about 3⁄16" (5mm).

AFFIXING THE ELASTIC TUBING

Threading the elastic tubing through the holes can be tricky. If you decide to use tweezers or a similar implement, it is important not to make any tears in the ends, as even a small tear can cause the tubing to split. Inspect the ends carefully before pushing the wooden dowels into each end of tubing, leaving about ⁵⁄₁₆" (8mm) of the dowel visible. Then pull through each strand of tubing and test the strength of the assembly by extending the tubing fully and holding the leather pouch as if you were ready to aim and release a charge.

FINISHING TOUCHES

By this stage of the project, you should feel a sense of accomplishment for finding a suitably shaped branch and for making it into a working slingshot. Adding a length of leather lace through a hole at the end of the handle is not essential, but it finishes it off neatly and provides a useful way of displaying your work.

DISCLAIMER
The Publisher and Author cannot be held responsible for any injury or accidents caused by slingshots. Even though slingshots are not restricted items, children should always be supervised by adults if allowed to use them, and they should be kept out of reach of children. When using a slingshot, always know your target and what's behind it. Do not shoot at hard surfaces or at the surface of water. Slingshot ammunition may bounce off or ricochet and hit someone or something you had not intended to hit.

JUMP ROPE

Jump rope, or skipping rope, is probably one of the easiest ways to enjoy exercise for a wide range of ages, but it is not seen so much in children's playgrounds today as it was in the past. A popular activity, particularly with girls or in groups of three or more, it was often accompanied by rhymes while jumping. The ends of the rope were turned by two non-skippers while one or more people skipped to the beat of a sung verse or chant. Many professional trainers, fitness experts, and professional fighters recommend using a jump rope for burning fat over any other exercises, such as running and jogging. Not only is this simple project a good introduction to working with coppiced wood, but it might also encourage you to take up an exercise that can be done indoors or out.

TOOLS
Bench Vise, Pull Saw, Cordless Drill, Tenon Cutter, Bench Hook, ⅜" (10mm) Brad Point Woodworking Bit, Sanding Block

MATERIALS
Ash, Hazel, Beech, Sycamore, Yew, Cherry, Oak, or Birch
10' (3m) of ⁵⁄₁₆" (8mm) diameter Rope

SELECTING THE WOOD

For this project, you will need some clean and reasonably smooth lengths of coppiced hardwood that can be used to form handles that can be held comfortably.

CUTTING TO LENGTH

To provide a good grip, the lengths of coppiced hardwood for the handles are likely to be thick, so a pull saw with medium teeth is the best choice—a pull saw with fine teeth can easily get jammed, especially if the moisture content of the wood is high. The length of the handles can be approximated by measuring them against the hand of the intended user but allowing an inch or so (a few centimeters) to make room for the shoulder.

CUTTING THE SHOULDER

This is a process where the tenon cutter comes into its own, as with careful practice it is capable of cutting a smooth, uninterrupted shoulder that no other tool can achieve. If you follow the detailed instructions included with each tool, you should achieve a near-perfect result (see page 36). The depth of cut can be measured and marked with a pencil so you can make both shoulders identical.

DRILLING

Drilling a clean hole down the center of the lengths of the handles is difficult but is easier if the central core of the coppiced hardwood is extremely soft, which can act as a guide.

The best type of drill for this is a brad point woodworking bit, which has a sharp, pointed end to prevent it accidentally moving when you begin the hole. The drill will need to be slightly thicker than the diameter of the rope, which in this case is $\frac{5}{16}$" (8mm), so if you are allowing for a clearance of $\frac{1}{16}$" (2mm), a $\frac{3}{8}$" (10mm) drill is needed.

The problem you might face when drilling a hole along the entirety of the handles is that a standard length of drill is unlikely to be long enough. It is therefore necessary to drill from both ends, so it is even more important that the handles are held securely and that the drill is in line.

FINISHING THE EDGES

Provided you are reasonably careful, this process can be done while resting the handles on the bench and sanding away from you. A neat edge prevents the wood from splintering while in use and gives a better finish to the completed product.

CHOOSING AND MEASURING THE ROPE

In this instance, I've chosen a length of brightly colored polyester rope, but there are many alternatives available in both synthetic and natural fibers. The correct length for an individual jump rope depends on your height. When you stand on the middle of the jump rope and pull both ends up toward the sky, the tips of the rope should reach your armpits. If the rope falls short of your armpits, it will not hit the ground as it passes under your feet when you jump. If the rope comes up well past your armpits, you may trip on the extra length, and it may become tangled as you jump.

FITTING THE ROPE

The fibrous nature of freshly coppiced wood can make it slightly difficult to thread the rope through the handles, but the clearance provided by using a larger-diameter drill compared to the diameter of the rope should be enough to make it pass easily. All that is needed now is a neatly tied knot to secure the rope.

TIP

If you've enjoyed making this project, you might like to try Double Dutch. This involves making two 13' (4m)-long jump ropes where two participants take one end of a rope in each hand and then spin them in opposite directions while a third participant stands in the middle and skips between the ropes.

CUP AND BALL

This is a game that has been around for years and is given different names by different cultures, each with their own interpretation of the basic idea. Essentially it is a game of skill in which the goal is to get the ball into the cup. Although the concept seems very easy, mastering it can sometimes be challenging. You will learn to improve your hand-eye coordination through making and then playing this game.

TOOLS
Bench Vise, Bench Hook, Cordless Drill, Pull Saw, Tenon Cutter, ¼" (6mm) Brad Point Woodworking Bit, Forstner Bit, Plastic-Faced Mallet, Sanding Block

MATERIALS
Ash, Beech, Sycamore, Cherry, Oak, or Birch
¼" (6mm) Dowel, Beech Ball, Thin Cord, Two-Part Epoxy Glue

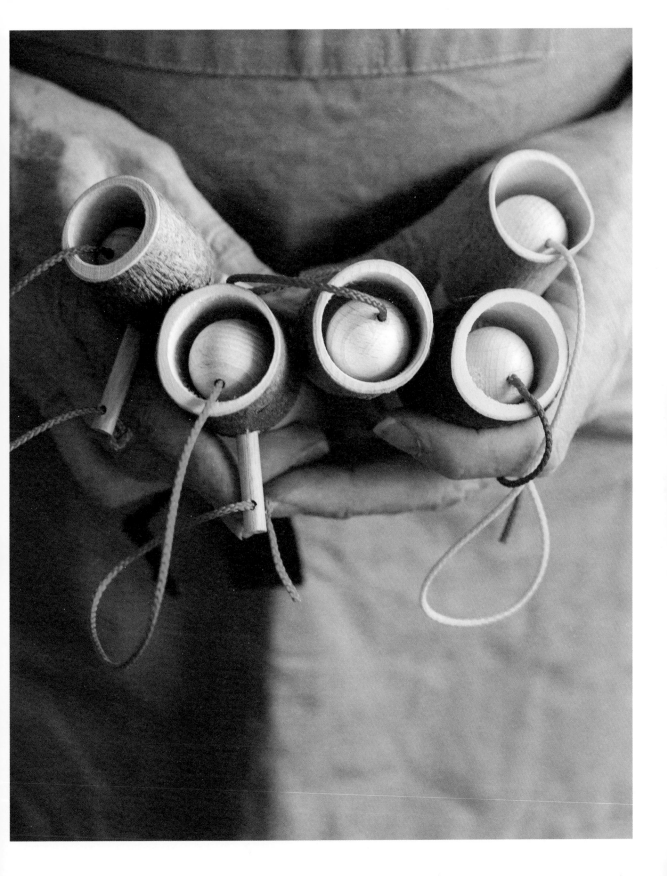

MAKING THE HANDLE

In this project, I have used a 1" (25mm) tenon cutter to form the handle and found that it works best when the greenwood has been freshly cut because it is much softer. Make sure the drill holding the tenon cutter is in line with the section of greenwood both from the side and top view and that it is held securely in the bench vise. Before you start the cut, the drill should be set to a slow speed, or, in the case of a variable speed drill, start slow and then increase the speed as the cut is made to form the tenon. This cut might need some practice before you make a tenon that is both straight and smooth.

Once you have successfully made a tenon to form the handle, the top section of the cup and ball can be separated by making a saw cut approximately 2" (50mm) above the shoulder.

DRILLING THE HOLES

To drill the top hole, you will need a forstner bit slightly smaller than the diameter of the greenwood. Once again begin the cut slowly and then increase the speed as the hole deepens to approximately 1⅝" (40mm).

Using a ¼" (6mm) brad point bit, drill the hole for the dowel slightly above the shoulder to a depth of approximately ⅜" (10mm).

ATTACHING THE DOWEL

Cut a short length of ¼" (6mm) dowel using the pull saw and bench hook, and then drill a small hole toward the end slightly larger than the diameter of the cord you've chosen.

Lightly smooth over the edges of both components and tap in the dowel with a plastic-faced mallet.

ATTACHING THE WOODEN BALL

Drill a second small hole slightly larger than the diameter of the cord you've chosen in the wooden ball. Using a two-part epoxy glue, carefully attach the cord to the wooden ball and leave to dry.

Pass the other end of the cord through the hole in the dowel and secure it with a knot.

TIP

There is also an opportunity with this project for you to adapt the proportions to either raise or lower the level of difficulty by increasing the diameter of the ball and cup accordingly.

WHISTLE

I found making a whistle that works to be difficult, and it took a number of attempts before I felt confident about the outcome. It seems that while any variety of hardwood is suitable, a clearer note can be achieved if the moisture content is lessened. This will only take a few weeks or even less if stored in a warm and dry environment, and for this purpose you should need a piece no thicker than your thumb. I've added a leather lanyard attached to a brass split ring, both of which can be bought from a shoe repairer. Don't be disappointed if at first you don't succeed, and don't be surprised when you do succeed with the volume and pitch of the note.

TOOLS
Bench Vise, ¾" (19mm) Tenon Cutter, Cordless Drill, Japanese Fine-Toothed Pull Saw, Bench Hook, Wide Single-Bevel Carpenter's Chisel, Small Round Rasp, Sanding Block, 5⁄16" (8mm) Brad Point Woodworking Bit, Countersink Bit

MATERIALS
Ash, Hazel, Beech, Sycamore, Yew, Cherry, Oak, or Birch
5⁄16" (8mm) Beech Dowel, Two-Part Epoxy Glue, Brass Split Ring, Length of Leather Lace

CUTTING THE MOUTHPIECE

Here I've used a tenon cutter, which makes for a smooth and pleasing mouthpiece, but you could carve this shape with a knife if one wasn't available. Tenon cutters come in different sizes, and the one pictured here is an example of a larger model. Smaller ones are available, but you would have to adjust the thickness of the dowel accordingly. See the instructions on page 36 for cutting a tenon.

DRILLING

Care needs to be taken to secure the work in the vise before attempting to drill through the tenon. It is important that both the drill and the work are in alignment from both the top and side before you begin, as the purpose is to drill a hole down the center using the brad point bit. This might take some practice at first but can be helped if someone at the side gives you instructions. The depth of the hole can be adjusted later, but it should be at least deep enough to allow for the notch.

CROSS CUT

You'll need a sharp, fine-toothed saw to make this cut, which should be made as far down as halfway through the hole, but no further. One way of accurately calculating the depth is to insert a piece of waste and gently make the cut until you can feel the waste turn around in your hand.

CUTTING THE WINDOW

Remove the work from the vise and hold it firmly against the top edge of the bench hook. You can then slowly and carefully pare away thin sections of waste with a wide and sharp chisel until you reach the point where the bottom of the saw cut reaches halfway through the hole.

THE FIPPLE

To make a sound from your whistle, the next thing to prepare is what is known as the fipple. This fipple is made by taking a section of 5⁄16" (8mm) dowel and paring away the top edge to form a smooth taper in the same way as you cut the notch. You can now see if you can make a sound by inserting the fipple so it goes no further than the notch and adjusting it until a sound is produced. The pitch of the whistle can be deepened by increasing the depth of the hole. Once done, the fipple can be glued into place and cut to size.

CUTTING THE END

This requires four cuts, with two going across and the other two going down. The two going across are cut with a small rasp parallel to each other on opposite sides. The depth of the cuts are roughly the diameter of the small rasp. Instead of using a small rasp, it could be replaced by a saw cut and then rounded into shape with some abrasive paper wrapped around a round object. The work should then be turned around in the vise so that two parallel saw cuts can be made to remove the waste.

FINISHING

Even if you use a fine saw for these cuts, it will leave a rough surface, so both sides need to be smoothed down with the sanding block and then the ends rounded over and given a chamfer to prevent splintering. Next, drill a hole large enough to take the split ring so it can move freely. For this purpose it is best to use a brad point woodworking drill. When drilling this hole, the work should be firmly held against the surface of the bench hook. When the point of the drill appears on the opposite side, stop drilling and turn the work over to complete the process to produce a clean hole. Lastly, use the countersink bit to finish the edges.

ATTACHING A LANYARD

The lanyard can now be attached to your whistle with a split ring, which in this case has been made from brass.

PING PONG PADDLES

Ping pong is the sort of bat and ball game that can be played at any age, and depending on the type of ball, it can be played both indoors and out. Nobody knows where it originated, but it seems that even the ancients had some version of it, which in turn led to the diverse number of interpretations found in every corner of the world. This project not only uses unseasoned hardwood but manufactured board, too, which makes an interesting contrast between the extremes.

TOOLS

Bench Vise, Ruler, Pencil, Bench Hook, Pull Saw, Cordless Drill, Coping Saw, Small Round Rasp, Sanding Block, Compass, Brad Point Woodworking Bit, Countersink Bit

MATERIALS

Ash, Hazel, Beech, Sycamore, Yew, Cherry, Oak, or Birch
¼" (6mm)-thick Manufactured Board, Countersunk Wood Screws

SELECTING THE WOOD

For this project, you'll not only need
lengths of unseasoned hardwood, but also
some offcuts of thin manufactured board
like plywood, about ¼" (6mm) thick. The
unseasoned hardwood should be thick
enough to form a comfortable handle for
the intended user, but the manufactured
board can be a matter of personal choice,
remembering that the level of difficulty is
related to the size of surface area.

CUTTING TO LENGTH

Once you've decided upon the intended user,
the lengths of unseasoned hardwood can be
measured and cut to size.

CUTTING THE JOINT

This process requires accurate cutting of a
slot in each of the handles in order to join
them securely to the faces. By holding the
edge of the board centrally against the end
of the handle, the saw cuts can be marked
with a sharp pencil and ruler. When you make
your incision, you should cut on the waste
side of the pencil line, as otherwise you will
not get a tight-fitting joint. To remove the
waste, you can either use the coping saw
or, as I have done, use a drill of the same
diameter as the thickness of the board.

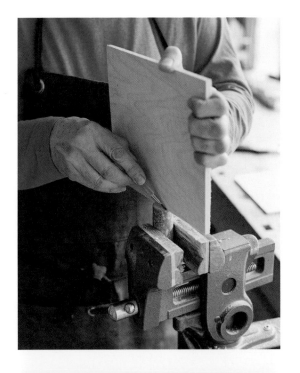

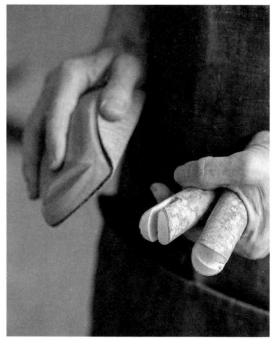

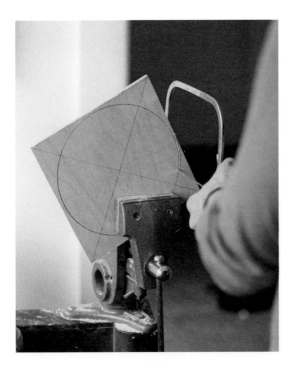

FINISHING THE HANDLES

Using a small rasp or some abrasive paper wrapped around some waste, the slots can be cleaned out, then with the sanding block the top edges and bottoms can be rounded over and chamfered to make a neat, smooth finish.

MARKING THE FACES

To find the center of the manufactured boards, use a ruler and pencil to draw in diagonals from opposite corners. Where the two lines cross, firmly place the point of the compass and carefully scribe the circle. If you don't have a compass, a round object like a plate could be used as a template.

CUTTING OUT THE FACES

One way to cut a circle by hand is with a coping saw, which has a narrow blade held under tension in a steel frame. It might take practice to achieve a clean cut, which is best made in short sections by holding it at right angles to the board. If the blade jams, try a gentler approach or change the blade by unscrewing the handle and replacing the old blade with a new one, making sure the teeth are pointing toward you.

FINISHING THE FACE EDGES

Provided you've made a reasonably accurate cut, only the minimum amount of waste should need to be removed to achieve a smooth, rounded edge.

The ball shown here was made from a length of rattan and was safe to use indoors as it was light but strong.

JOINING THE HANDLE TO THE FACE

To join the face to the handle of your paddle, you need to insert two small countersunk wood screws, preferably made from a noncorrosive material. These should be as narrow as possible and no longer than the thickness of the handle. Drill two clearance holes on only one side of the handle and then countersink them so they conceal the screw head. Next, make two more clearance holes in the face by placing it in the slot and marking the holes with a sharp pencil. You can now attach the two parts together and repeat the process for the second paddle.

DOG LEASH

This would make a lovely present for anyone who owns a dog, and is both practical and original—if you were feeling generous, you could also make them the whistle on page 118. This project also gives you the opportunity to combine the natural appearance of unseasoned hardwood with other elements like the rope and spring hook. Rope is available in synthetic and natural fibers, which both have their individual qualities and are equally strong. If you choose a synthetic fiber, you could add an exciting accent of color together with your choice of spring hook made from stainless steel, brass, or anodized aluminum.

TOOLS

Pull Saw, Bench Hook, Bench Vise, ¾" (19mm) Tenon Cutter, Sanding Block, Cordless Drill, ¹⁵⁄₃₂" (12mm) Brad Point Woodworking Bit

MATERIALS

Ash, Hazel, Beech, Sycamore, Yew, Cherry, Oak, or Birch
⅜" (10mm) diameter Rope, Spring Hook

DOG LEASH COMPONENTS

Whether you choose a synthetic rope or one made from a natural fiber like hemp or cotton, it needs to have three strands so you can join all three components together. Strength is another important consideration, so for this I'd recommend using rope with a diameter of ⅜" (10mm) and a heavy duty spring hook, which in this case is made from stainless steel. Lastly, the handle needs to be comfortable to hold and thick enough to take the rope.

CUTTING THE HANDLE TO SIZE

Before cutting the handle to size, you will need to decide on the length. This can be easily found by grasping a length of greenwood with your hand and marking accordingly, allowing extra for the shoulder. Once done, you can make the cut with the pull saw by holding the length of greenwood firmly against the bench hook.

CUTTING THE SHOULDER

Holding the length of greenwood in the bench vise, make a short cut with the tenon cutter, carefully following the instructions included with the tool.

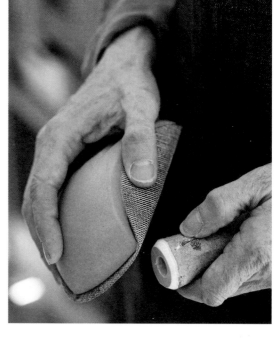

FINISHING THE EDGES

Using a sanding block fitted with medium grit abrasive paper, smooth over the edges of the the handle to avoid any splintering.

DRILLING THE HOLE

To drill this hole accurately, use a drill bit with a central point, as this will help guide the hole in the initial stage. The hole will need to be slightly bigger than the diameter of the rope, which in this case is ³⁄₈" (10mm)—so, allowing for a clearance of ³⁄₁₆" (2mm), a ¹⁵⁄₃₂" (12mm) diameter drill bit is needed. The problem you might face is that a standard drill is unlikely to be long enough, so it's necessary to drill from both ends and meet in the middle.

THREADING THE ROPE

Even though you have drilled a hole larger than the thickness of the rope, there are likely to be some greenwood fibers that need clearing out before you can thread it through. If the rope has frayed, this can cause a problem that can be easily solved by temporarily applying some tape around the end.

SPLICING

There are a number of different types of splices designed to join the ends of rope to stop it from fraying by untwisting and then interweaving the strands. (Detailed instruction for rope splicing can be found online.) For the purpose of joining the spring hook to the rope, we are going to splice it into a loop by holding it in the vise. Trim the ends of the completed splice with a sharp pair of scissors or a knife.

SPLICING THE HANDLE END

You will use the same splicing method here as you used when joining the spring hook, but this time make the loop larger so the hand can comfortably grip the handle. Trim the ends of the completed splice with a sharp pair of scissors or a knife.

TIP

If you choose a synthetic fiber, you could add an exciting accent of color together with your choice of spring hook made from stainless steel, brass, or anodized aluminum.

GLOSSARY

Bench Hook: A traditional device used to hold a piece of wood in position while it is cut.

Bench Vise: A vise affixed to the surface of a bench to hold irregular shaped pieces of material in place.

Brad Point Woodworking Bit: Precision ground drill bit with a single center point and twin outer cutting spurs.

Chamfer: A symmetrical sloping edge of a piece of timber.

Coping Saw: A saw with a very narrow blade stretched across a D-shaped frame, used for cutting curves in wood.

Coppicing: A traditional woodland management technique of cutting back a tree to encourage new growth.

Countersink Bit: A tool used to allow a wood screw to be flush with the surface of the material.

Dowel: A cylindrical wooden rod often used to join pieces together, either to align them or to prevent them from slipping.

Forstner Bit: A woodworking drill bit that is guided by the outside rim. It is useful when drilling angled holes.

Greenwood: Freshly cut wood with a high moisture content.

Hardwood: Hardwoods come from broad-leaved, deciduous trees.

Japanese Saw: Japanese saws are designed to cut on the pull stroke, allowing for a cleaner cut, which allows the cutting width to be smaller and more controlled.

Mortise and Tenon: A type of joint that connects two pieces of wood or other materials together. A mortise is a recess cut into wood to fit a tenon, a tongue at the end of a piece of wood that slots into the mortise.

Plastic-Faced Mallet: This is capable of supplying firm, heavy blows while limiting damage to the item being struck. The faces are designed to wear and can be replaced.

Pull Saw: A handsaw used to cut small sections of wood.

Tenon Cutter: A unique tool used to make a round tenon.

Sanding Block: A block used to hold a sanding disc for sanding.

Sanding Discs: A disc used to sand wood. They are available in different sizes.

Single-Bevel Carpenter's Chisel: This features a long, flat, thin blade that tapers toward the cutting edge to give a fine cut.

Small Round Rasp: These rasps are used to cut with precision and don't scrape or tear the wood.

Softwood: Softwoods come from evergreen, needle-leaved, cone-bearing conifers, such as cedar, fir, and pine.

Splicing: A way of terminating a rope or joining two ends of rope together without using a knot.

Two-Part Epoxy Glue: A very strong two-part adhesive used to join different types of materials together.

Variable Speed Cordless Drill: A battery-powered drill that can change speed by applying pressure to the power trigger.

INDEX

I mentioned earlier in this book the collaboration I have with Marianne Lumholdt and Mark Bedford of Mar Mar Co, who were the first retailers to introduce my work to the general public. In parallel to their retail business, they run a graphic design studio, and it was an obvious and appropriate choice for me that they should be the designers of this book. This collaboration has lasted more than five years, and during that time we have never worked harder together than on this book, so it not only provides the reader with a clear description of the projects, but together with the photography of Sarah Weal and Jake Curtis is hopefully a pleasure to own or pass on. Many others have also contributed both directly and indirectly to the making of this book, and I'd like to acknowledge the support of the following:

Alan Russell – *R. Russell Brushes*; Allison O'Connor– *Williams Sonoma Agrarian*; Barry Pratt; Cliff Rayner – *Isaac Lords*; Craig Townsley and Paula Webb – *Axminster Tools*; Craig Brown – *Sporting Wholesale*; Emily Lambert – *SeedBall*; Gina Marris –*The New Craftsmen*; Helen Cathcart – *Helen Cathcart Photography*; Ian Parr – *Chatham Rope Company*; Ian Wright – *Allport Packaging*; Isaac Lords Limited; Jude King; Jake Curtis – *Jake Curtis Photography*; Judith Hannam – *Kyle Books*; Jane Akers – *Homes and Gardens*; Jack Neville – *Jack Neville Photography*; John Shaw – *Chiltern Rangers*; Kelvin Green; Lewis and Laurence Mitchell – *Really Well Made*; Lisa Lee Benjamin – *Evo Catalyst*; Labour and Wait; Laurie Spicer and Adrian Dent – *Department of International Trade*; Laurie Gear – *The Artichoke*; Marianne Lumholdt and Mark Bedford – *Mar Mar Co*; Marie Ballantine – *Margaret Howell*; Mary Claire Smith – *Frank*; Nina Allen – *Sweet Bella USA*; Olivia Clemence and Zoe Laughlin – *Institute of Making UCL*; Phil Schramm; Phillip Eccles; Richard and Jan Mash; Rosie Forsyth – *Wilkins Accountants*; Robin Horton – *Urban Gardens*; Robert Penn; Richard Bennett; Simon Alderson – *Twenty Twentyone*; Sarah Lonsdale and Michelle Slatalla – *Remodelista*; Sarah Weal – *Sarah Weal Photography*; Sarah Henry; Studiomama; The Woodland Trust; Tracey Clarke – *The Craft Council*; Tricia Hylton.

First published in Great Britain in 2018 by Kyle Books, an imprint of Kyle Cathie Limited, part of Octopus Publishing Group Ltd, Carmelite House, 50 Victoria Embankment, London EC4Y 0DZ

This version published by Fox Chapel Publishing Company, Inc., 903 Square Street, Mount Joy, PA 17552.

Text copyright 2018 © Geoffrey Fisher

Design and layout copyright 2018 © Kyle Cathie Ltd

Photographs copyright 2018 © Sarah Weal except pp 2, 4, 6, 8, 11, 12, 15, 16, 19, 20 (top left, top right, bottom left), 23, 24, 25, 72, 73, 95, 96, 97, 98, 99, 100 and 101 copyright 2018 © Jake Curtis

ISBN 978-1-4971-0004-6

Editorial Director: Judith Hannam
Editorial Assistant: Isabel Gonzalez-Prendergast
Designer: Mar Mar Co. Studio
Photographer: Jake Curtis and Sarah Weal
Production: Lisa Pinnell
Americanization for US Edition: Colleen Dorsey

The Cataloging-in-Publication Data is on file with the Library of Congress.

To learn more about the other great books from Fox Chapel Publishing, or to find a retailer near you, call toll-free 800-457-9112 or visit us at *www.FoxChapelPublishing.com.*

We are always looking for talented authors. To submit an idea, please send a brief inquiry to acquisitions@foxchapelpublishing.com.

Printed in China

10 9 8 7 6 5 4 3 2 1

DISCLAIMER
The Publisher and Author cannot be held responsible for any injury or accidents caused by slingshots. Even though slingshots are not restricted items, children should always be supervised by adults if allowed to use them, and they should be kept out of reach of children. When using a slingshot, always know your target and what's behind it. Do not shoot at hard surfaces or at the surface of water. Slingshot ammunition may bounce off or ricochet and hit someone or something you had not intended to hit.